THE LITTLE GUIDE TO

CHANEL

First published in 2026 by OH
An Imprint of HEADLINE PUBLISHING GROUP

1

Disclaimer:
This book has not been licensed, approved, sponsored, or endorsed by Chanel or any rightsholder(s) in respect of this brand.

Chanel is a registered trademark owned by Chanel, Inc.

Cataloguing in Publication Data is available from the British Library

ISBN 978-1-03543-651-4

Compiled and written by Katie Meegan
Editorial: Beth Bishop
Designed and typset in Avenir by Stephen Cary
Project manager: Russell Porter
Production: Rachel Burgess
Printed and bound in Dubai

MIX
Paper | Supporting
responsible forestry
FSC
www.fsc.org   FSC® C104740

Headline's policy is to use papers that are natural, renewable and recyclable products and made from wood grown in well-managed forests and other controlled sources. The logging and manufacturing processes are expected to conform to the environmental regulations of the country of origin.

HEADLINE PUBLISHING GROUP LIMITED
An Hachette UK Company
Carmelite House, 50 Victoria Embankment, London EC4Y 0DZ

The authorized representative in the EEA is Hachette Ireland, 8 Castlecourt Centre, Dublin 15, D15 XTP3, Ireland (email: info@hbgi.ie)

www.headline.co.uk   www.hachette.co.uk

THE LITTLE GUIDE TO

CHANEL

STYLE TO LIVE BY

Unofficial and Unauthorized

OH

CONTENTS

INTRODUCTION

Where the House of Chanel goes, the world of fashion follows. Home to not one, but two of the greatest designers to ever have lived – the eponymous founder Coco Chanel and the iconic Karl Lagerfeld – Chanel has remained at the forefront of contemporary design for over a century.

Gabrielle "Coco" Chanel began as a milliner before expanding into sports clothing, experimenting with jersey – a relatively cheap fabric typically used for men's underwear. While initially dismissed as "boyish" and a "poor girl" look, her practical and comfortable yet elegant designs soon gathered admirers among upper-class women, desperate to be freed from the constraints of the corset.

From there came the little black dress, incredibly versatile and chic – still a staple in any fashionista's wardrobe today – as well as the iconic Chanel accessories: strings of pearls, costume jewellery, the camelia flower, the two-tone shoe. Chanel retreated from the world of design during World War II –

re-emerging during the 1950s to reclaim her place as the queen of chic. Throughout Chanel's second act she continued to create elegant pieces for the modern woman, including the famous Chanel two-piece tweed suit and the 2.55 bag. She died in 1971.

The House of Chanel's next imagining came from German-born designer Karl Lagerfeld. Having revolutionized lines at both Chloé and Fendi, Lagerfeld was a surprising choice to spearhead the heritage House of Chanel, however, today he is as synonymous with Chanel as Coco herself. Lagerfeld turned runway shows into awe-inspiring performances, re-focusing on Coco's vision of the "whole look", mixing archival designs with innovative offerings and reinstating Chanel as a "must-have" brand throughout the 1980s to the late 2010s.

From the flappers of the jazz age to modern-day celebrities, the House of Chanel continues to be a beacon of elegance, innovation and, ultimately, fashion itself.

CHAPTER
ONE

FROM COCO
TO CHANEL

THERE IS NO CHANEL
WITHOUT COCO. FROM HUMBLE
BEGINNINGS AS A MILLINER,
COCO CHANEL LIBERATED
WOMEN FROM THE CONSTRAINTS
OF CORSETS, MELDING LUXURY,
ELEGANCE AND COMFORT
IN A TRULY GROUNDBREAKING
FASHION.

Born in 1883 into poverty, Gabrielle "Coco" Chanel was abandoned on the front steps of a convent at the age of just 11 by her father upon her mother's death.

It was in this convent that she learnt dressmaking, before becoming a café singer. Known for her charisma and sharp wit, Chanel secured financial backing from a wealthy lover in order to open a small millinery shop.

> "
>
> Fashion is not something that exists in dresses only. Fashion is in the sky, in the street, fashion has to do with ideas, the way we live, what is happening.
>
> "

Coco Chanel

On her definition of fashion, harpersbazaar.com, 7 July 2021

66

Luxury must be comfortable, otherwise it is not luxury.

99

Coco Chanel

Her mantra, which was at odds with the corset-led fashion of the time, harpersbazaar.com, 27 August 2021

"

The popular image of Chanel is of a unique genius who created her personal style in isolation from other designers, and virtually single-handedly brought women into the modern era.

"

Valerie Steele

Fashion historian, on Chanel's revolutionary approach to women's wear, *The Collection Museum at the Fashion Institute of Technology: Fashion Designers A-Z*, Valerie Steele, 2018

When World War I broke out in 1914, Coco Chanel was poised to take the lead on a new form of fashion.

As women took on more active roles and luxury materials became scare, Chanel's practical, relaxed designs, free from the constraints of corsets and wide skirts, became increasingly popular with both aristocracy and middle classes alike.

"

I gave women a sense of freedom;
I gave them back their bodies:
bodies that were drowned in
finery, lace, frills, feathers, and
fripperies.

"

Coco Chanel

On her purpose, chanel.com, 7 July 2025

66

Don't spend time beating on
a wall, hoping to transform it into
a door.

99

Coco Chanel

On where to focus your energy, harpersbazaar.com,
27 August 2021

The 1920s was the decade of Chanel. Her corset-less and comfortable dresses became synonymous with the "flapper" aesthetic of the emerging jazz age.

Often paired with costume jewellery and strings of pearls, the Chanel look was popular across Europe and America.

##

66

Elegance is refusal.

99

Coco Chanel

On her core aesthetic principle, harpersbazaar.com, 7 July 2021

66

Fashion fades, only style remains the same.

99

Coco Chanel

On the importance of timeless style, harpersbazaar.com, 27 August 2021

In 1926, *Vogue* published a drawing of Chanel's simple, straight black dress, dubbing it "Chanel's Ford" – a reference to its universal appeal and streamlined design, much like the Ford Model T car.

This moment is often cited as the birth of the modern "Little Black Dress", solidifying its place as a wardrobe staple for decades to come.

"

A uniform for all women
of taste.

"

Vogue

From a 1926 article heralding the invention of Chanel's Little
Black Dress, as seen in *The Ten: The Stories Behind The Fashion
Classics*, Lauren Cochrane, 2021

> **Black has it all. White too.
> Their beauty is absolute. It is the
> perfect harmony.**

Coco Chanel

On her masterful use of black and white – colours synonymous
with early Chanel, chanel.com, 7 July 2025

66

Fashion should die and die quickly, in order that commerce may survive.

Coco Chanel

As seen in *The Allure of Chanel,* Paul Morand, 1976

99

As the roaring twenties faded and the world slid into the global economic downturn of the 1930s, Chanel continued to innovate, introducing more sophisticated evening wear and expanding into jewellery and cosmetics.

> **"**
>
> You were born an original, don't become a copy.
>
> **"**

Coco Chanel

On identity, wwd.com, 27 August 2024

"

Fit to rule a man and an empire.

"

Winston Churchill

On Coco Chanel in a letter to his wife, theguardian.com,
10 September 2023

As World War II approached, Coco Chanel controversially closed her Parisian fashion house in 1939, maintaining only her perfume and accessories lines.

Her actions during the war, including her alleged love affair with a Nazi officer, later became a significant and complex chapter in her personal and professional history.

“

I only drink Champagne on two occasions: when I am in love and when I am not.

”

Coco Chanel

Chanel had numerous high-profile love affairs throughout her life, harpersbazaar.com, 7 July 2021

"

Chanel was of her times, an opportunist and a survivor, which probably influenced her choices.

"

Hannah Berryman

Filmmaker and director of *Coco Chanel Unbuttoned*, theguardian.com, 10 September 2023

Despite the wartime closure of her couture house, the Chanel No. 5 fragrance continued to thrive, particularly in the American market.

This enduring success provided a financial lifeline and maintained the brand's global presence even as the head of the house remained on an indefinite hiatus.

"

In order to be irreplaceable one must always be different.

"

Coco Chanel

On reputation, harpersbazaar.com, 7 July 2021

66

A woman is closest to being naked when she is well dressed.

99

Coco Chanel

On dressing well, harpersbazaar.com, 27 August 2021

The end of World War II marked a period of introspection and recovery for Coco Chanel.

Her fashion house remained closed after the liberation of Paris, and she retreated from public view for several years.

However, in true Chanel style, she shocked critics and customers alike with a surprise return to couture in the mid-1950s.

CHAPTER
TWO

A HOUSE REBORN

FROM THE ASHES OF WORLD
WAR II ROSE A NEW HOUSE OF
CHANEL, WITH THE TIRELESS
COCO STILL AT THE HELM,
FIRMLY MAKING HER PRESENCE
KNOWN IN THE BOOMING
POST-WAR PARISIAN HAUTE
COUTURE SCENE.

EVER THE SYMBOL OF FRENCH
REFINEMENT AND ELEGANCE,
HER DESIGNS CONTINUED
TO ADORN EVERYONE FROM FIRST
LADIES TO BRITISH ROYALTY.

After a 15-year hiatus from the world of fashion, Coco Chanel made a daring return in 1954 at the age of 71.

French press was sceptical of her comeback at the time, preferring to endorse a "new" generation of designers including the likes of Christian Dior, but the American and British markets rejoiced at the return of the queen of couture.

Because I was dying of boredom.

Coco Chanel

Her reported reply to close friend Marlène Dietrich when
the actress asked why she was returning to fashion,
classicchiagomagazine.com, 14 July 2025

> "

Here is a woman who created her own company in the early twentieth century, was a super-successful businesswoman, who never married, and fought for her own economic freedom. She may not have called herself a feminist, but she made huge contributions to women's history in the twentieth century.

"

Miren Arzalluz

Museum director and co-curator of *Gabrielle Chanel: Fashion Manifesto*, thebbc.com, 2 February 2021

Chanel's returning collection in 1954 initially received a lukewarm reception in Paris, with critics finding it too conservative in comparison to Dior's "New Look".

However, her classic, comfortable and practical designs resonated strongly with women seeking sophisticated, wearable clothes – particularly in the American market.

"

Dior doesn't dress women.
He upholsters them.

"

Coco Chanel

On Christian Dior – her post-war Parisian fashion rival,
who she often claimed was trying to drag women backwards with
his corsetry and flamboyant style, elledecor.com,
12 February 2024

"

Simplicity is the keynote of
all true elegance.

"

Coco Chanel

On her unwavering aesthetic, harpersbazaar.com, 7 July 2021

"

Dress shabbily and they remember the dress; dress impeccably and they remember the woman.

"

Coco Chanel

On the importance of first impressions, harpersbazaar.com, 27 August 2021

The tailored suit was the hallmark of Chanel's post-war collections. The classic Chanel suit, still to this day, is characterized by its collarless, braid-trimmed jacket, fitted skirt and comfortable tweed fabric.

The suit offered a chic yet functional alternative to the prevalent hourglass silhouettes of Dior's "New Look", becoming a symbol of contemporary femininity and power.

"

The Chanel suit is not just a uniform, it is a second skin for the woman who wears it.

"

Coco Chanel

On the enduring design of her signature suit, chanel.com, 7 July 2025

"

The most courageous act is still
to think for yourself. Aloud.

"

Coco Chanel

On self-worth, townandcountrymag.com, 16 August 2017

Coco Chanel's later years were marked by her continuous creative output, meticulously overseeing every detail of her collections from her suite at the Hôtel Ritz in Paris.

Coco remained a formidable and exacting figure, fiercely protective of her brand's identity and her vision of understated elegance.

"

A girl should be two things:
classy and fabulous.

"

Coco Chanel

On the most important attributes, townandcoutrymag.com,
16 August 2017

66

She survived them all… She wasn't only a designer – she was a woman of her time.

99

Karl Lagerfeld

On Coco Chanel's formidable presence in her later years, vogue.co.uk, 11 November 2010

Coco Chanel passed away in her apartment on 10 January 1971 at the age of 87. She continued to design right up to her death.

Her passing left a profound void in the fashion world and raised questions as to the future of the House of Chanel without its iconic founder.

66

You can be gorgeous at 30, charming at 40, and irresistible for the rest of your life.

99

Coco Chanel

On aging, harpersbazaar.com, 7 July 2021

"

Dress like you are going to meet your worst enemy today.

"

Coco Chanel

On power dressing, wwd.com, 27 August 2024

"

If you're sad, add more lipstick
and attack.

"

Coco Chanel

On the power of lipstick, townandcountrymag,com,
16 August 2017

"

I built my house on black, white and beige. These colours are the foundation of my style, the perfect backdrop for everything else.

"

Coco Chanel

On her core colour palette, chanel.com, accessed 7 July 2025

"

Nature gives you the face you have at 20. Life shapes the face you have at 30. But at 50 you get the face you deserve.

"

Coco Chanel

On aging, harpersbazaar.com, 27 August 2021

Following the death of Coco Chanel, the House of Chanel continued to operate under the leadership of a handful of her trusted associates.

The brand's focus largely shifted to its profitable perfume and accessories divisions during this transitional period, which raised an important question in Paris and beyond – would Chanel ever return to couture?

66

I don't do fashion. I am fashion.

Coco Chanel

On her identity and influence, harpersbazaar.com, 7 July 2021

99

"

Some people think luxury is
the opposite of poverty. It is not.
It is the opposite of vulgarity.

"

Coco Chanel

On luxury, wwd.com, 27 August 2024

"

My life didn't please me,
so I created my life.

"

Coco Chanel

On building her fashion empire and legacy,
townandcountrymag.com, 16 August 2017

"

You live but once; you might
as well be amusing.

"

Coco Chanel

On living fully, harpersbazaar.com, 7 July 2021

"

She dedicated her life to imagining a new way for women to experience fashion.

"

Miren Arzalluz

Fashino museum curator, on the legacy of Coco Chanel, 2 February 2021

"

A woman who cuts her hair is about to change her life.

"

Coco Chanel

The founder was famous for her "tomboyish" bob,
townandcountrymag.com, 16 August 2017

"

Chanel freed women.

"

Yves Saint Laurent

Admirer and fellow couturier, irishexaminer.com,
16 February 2014

By the 1980s, the owners of Chanel, the Wertheimer family, had recognized the need for a significant revitalization and began to seek a designer who could inject new life into the historic fashion house.

This search would ultimately lead to a pivotal appointment that would forever change Chanel's trajectory – Karl Lagerfeld.

CHAPTER
THREE

THE LAGERFELD YEARS

KARL LAGERFELD WAS A
VISIONARY WHO REVIVED AND
REIMAGINED CHANEL FOR THE
MODERN ERA, TRANSFORMING
THE SLEEPY HERITAGE BRAND
INTO A GLOBAL POWERHOUSE
SYNONYMOUS WITH
INNOVATION AND SPECTACLE.

MUCH LIKE COCO CHANEL,
HE WAS AN ICON – STANDING
OUT ON THE GLOBAL STAGE
FOR BOTH HIS PERSONAL STYLE
AND DESIGN GENIUS.

Born in Hamburg in 1933, Karl Lagerfeld was the son of an evaporated milk entrepreneur. He was close to his mother, Elisabeth, and credited her with his initial interest in fashion.

Lagerfeld often felt conflicted about his German upbringing, moving to Paris as a teenager to pursue a career in fashion. He worked at Balmain, Fendi and Chloé before being approached for the top job at Chanel at the age of 50.

66

I am a fashion person, and fashion is not only about clothes – it's about all kinds of change.

99

Karl Lagerfeld

On the importance of his industry, harpersbazaar.com,
19 February 2020

"

When I started working at Chanel about 30 years ago, people told me not to touch it, it's dead, and it won't come back. But that's actually the main reason why I accepted – there is nothing better than a challenge.

"

Karl Lagerfeld

On the challenge of revitalizing the brand, system-magazine.com, 19 November 2024

Lagerfeld's initial challenge was to modernize Chanel without alienating its loyal, traditional clientele, while simultaneously attracting a new, younger audience.

He immersed himself in Coco Chanel's archives, meticulously studying her designs before embarking on his radical reinterpretation.

"

35 years ago, old labels were old labels. Now everybody wants to revive a label, and some of them, I don't think it's a good idea. But this was before Tom Ford and Gucci.

"

Karl Lagerfeld

On how his work with Chanel became the blueprint for rival brand revivals, thecut.com, 9 December 2018

"

I play with Chanel's elements like a musician plays with notes. You don't have to make the same music if you are a decent musician.

"

Karl Lagerfeld

On his mission at the house, vogue.co.uk, 11 November 2010

66

[Lagerfeld] committed too
many Chanel Don'ts and not
enough Do's.

99

Women's Wear Daily

A less-than-flattering 1983 headline, showing how Lagerfeld
strived to maintain the legacy of Chanel while bring it into a new
era, theguardian.com, 19 February 2019

Lagerfeld's early collections for Chanel were met with both excitement and controversy.

He boldly played with Chanel's iconic tweed, chains, pearls and camellias, often subverting them with unexpected twists, punk influences and a youthful energy that shocked Chanel's core audience but captivated a cooler new market.

"

For the 1987 collections, the photographers were bad. Eric Pfrunder the image director shot the collection three times with different photographers, and it still was not very good. Then he told me, 'If it is that complicated, we should do it ourselves.'

"

Karl Lagerfeld

On how he also became a photographer at Chanel, system-magazine.com, 19 November 2024

"

You can only really build something new if you destroy the old.

"

Karl Lagerfeld

On reinventing Chanel, anothermag.com, 21 June 2019

Under Lagerfeld, Chanel's runway shows became legendary spectacles, transforming the Grand Palais into fantastical worlds – from supermarkets and rocket launches to enchanted forests and beaches.

These elaborate sets became as famous as the collections themselves, generating immense media buzz and cementing Chanel's cultural relevance throughout the 1980s and well into the 2010s.

66

Fashion is a language that creates itself in clothes to interpret reality.

99

Karl Lagerfeld

On fashion's role as a mirror to society, gq.com,
19 February 2019

"

The Chanel supermarket show was a pivotal moment. It proved fashion could be smart, witty, and incredibly relevant to popular culture, not just an elite art form.

"

Tim Blanks

Fashion commentator, on the impact of Lagerfeld's conceptual shows, businessoffashion.com, 4 March 2014

Lagerfeld was a prolific designer, often presenting eight collections a year for Chanel across haute couture, ready-to-wear and resort.

His relentless creativity ensured Chanel remained at the forefront of fashion, constantly introducing new iterations of the house codes while pushing stylistic boundaries.

"

I am a kind of fashion ventilator.

"

Karl Lagerfeld

Describing his constant flow of ideas, interviewmagazine.com,
1 October 2010

66

Before, fashion was easy, in a way,
There was the couture collection...
that was the fashion in the world.
Now fashion comes from the street,
from other designers, from ready-
to-wear, so high fashion has to be
the fashion of the moment.

99

Karl Lagerfeld

Explaining why a shift in Chanel's aesthetics was necessary in the
1980s, newyorker.com, 12 March 2007

Beyond clothing, Lagerfeld expanded Chanel's accessories empire, introducing new versions of the classic 2.55 bag, innovative costume jewellery and iconic footwear that became instant bestsellers.

These accessible luxury items significantly contributed to the brand's global commercial success.

"

A collection is not just one basic idea. It comes from something that is in the air, something you suddenly like... People today are so used to taking one theme and staying with it all the way. I don't do that... I'm more interested in working out technical ideas than I am in themes.

"

Karl Lagerfeld

On his inspirations, interviewmagazine.com, 27 April 2009

❝

Some designers are very elitist, and, though Karl was a snob in some ways, he was also very democratic. He wanted to appeal to the world – I mean, he wanted everyone to come to his party.

❞

Anna Wintour

Fashion editor, on Lagerfeld's populist appeal, *Paradise Now: The Extraordinary Life of Karl Lagerfeld*, William Middleton, 2023

Lagerfeld's creative influence extended beyond design to the brand's image, photography and advertising.

A gifted photographer, he often shot Chanel's campaigns himself, working with top models and celebrities, further shaping the brand's powerful and aspirational identity in the global consciousness.

"

I shoot with my eyes. And with my instinct.

"

Karl Lagerfeld

On his approach to photography, gq.com, 19 February 2019

66

Karl was a genius and always so kind and generous to me both personally and professionally.

99

Victoria Beckham

Recalling when she posed for Lagerfeld at a 2012 photoshoot in Paris, harpersbazaar.com, 21 June 2019

Throughout his long tenure, Lagerfeld maintained a strong public persona, characterized by his distinctive uniform of a white ponytail, dark suit and sunglasses.

He became an icon in his own right, inextricably linked with the revitalization and global dominance of Chanel. He was a stalwart of the 1990s supermodel era, with any and every supermodel worth their salt walking for Chanel.

“

I am like a caricature of myself,
and I like that. It is like a mask.
And for me the Carnival of Venice
lasts all year long.

”

Karl Lagerfeld

On his public image, harpersbazaar.com, 19 February 2020

"

Karl's support transformed me from a shy German teenager into a supermodel. As intuitive as he was innovative, his advice, wit and inexhaustible energy were infectious and inspiring in equal measure. To his muse, he was my mentor, a profoundly cultured, kind and charismatic man.

"

Claudia Schiffer

Model, actor and Chanel catwalk regular in the 1990s, vogue.co.uk, 23 February 2019

Karl Lagerfeld passed away on 19 February 2019, at the age of 85.

His death marked the end of an unparalleled 36-year tenure at Chanel, leaving behind a legacy of innovation, spectacle and the astonishing transformation of the historic French house into a modern luxury powerhouse.

"

My greatest luxury is not to have
to justify myself to anyone.

Karl Lagerfeld

Reflecting on his autonomy and creative freedom,
interviewmagazine.com, 1 October 2010

"

"

He didn't just save Chanel; he made it bigger, bolder and more culturally relevant than Coco ever could have imagined for the modern age.

"

Anna Wintour

Fashion editor, on Lagerfeld's immense legacy, vogue.com, 19 February 2019

"

I am never happy. Happiness scares me; then I am afraid to be less happy. Happiness is a very dangerous state of mind.

"

Karl Lagerfeld

On his motivations, of which happiness is not one, elle.com, September 2007

"

Why a supermarket? It is something of today's life and even people who dress at Chanel go there – it's a modern statement for expensive things.

"

Karl Lagerfeld

Explaining one of Chanel's most iconic moments: turning the Paris Grand Palais into a supermarket for a 2014 runway show, theguardian.com, 4 March 2014

Karl Lagerfeld, like Coco Chanel before him, remained the Head of the House of Chanel until his death in 2019.

Virginie Viard, his long-time right-hand woman and studio director, was immediately named as his successor, a testament to her many years working alongside the "master".

66

She is my right arm and
my left arm.

99

Karl Lagerfeld

On his trust and collaboration with Virginie Viard,
fashionnetwork.com, 6 June 2024

CHAPTER
FOUR

CHANEL TODAY

THE APPOINTMENT OF VIRGINIE VIARD WAS A SURPRISE TO NO ONE, AND UNDER HER, THE HOUSE SAW A RETURN TO THE LUXURIOUS SIMPLICITY OF CHANEL'S PAST.

WITH MATTHIEU BLAZY NOW AT THE HELM, CHANEL IS AT THE START OF A BOLD NEW ERA, WHERE ITS CLASSIC CODES ARE FACING COMPLETE REINVENTION FOR THE MODERN FASHION WORLD. IN THE WORDS OF THE NEW YORK TIMES, THIS IS NOT YOUR GRANDMOTHER'S CHANEL...

Virginie Viard was appointed as Chanel's creative director following the passing of Karl Lagerfeld.

Viard's initial collections aimed to honour Lagerfeld's legacy while subtly introducing her own vision. She focused on lightening silhouettes, infusing a sense of youthful ease and a more relaxed femininity into the collections, often drawing inspiration from Coco Chanel's practical approach to dressing rather than Lagerfeld's showmanship.

66

I didn't want to be in the shadow
of Karl anymore. I wanted to
be myself.

99

Virginie Viard

On stepping into the spotlight, vogue.com, 27 May 2020

66

Life inspires me in general.

99

Virginie Viard

On her design philosophy, vogue.com, 27 April 2020

"

Our relationship is fundamental –
one of profound affection and a
true friendship.

"

Karl Lagerfeld

On the depth of his and Viard's relationship, highlighting how
naming her his successor was the natural choice, telegraph.co.uk,
20 February 2019

"

I like to think of myself as
the one who helps his vision
come alive.

"

Virginie Viard

On closely collaborating with Lagerfeld, theguardian.com,
27 May 2020

"

Viard, Karl Lagerfeld's long-term right-hand woman, has taken a softer, subtler approach since taking over after the legendary designer's death just over a year ago.

"

Hannah Marriott

Fashion critic, on Viard's shift in aesthetic, theguardian.com, 3 March 2020

For Chanel's runway shows, Viard drew inspiration from Coco Chanel's life and classic French cinema, creating a more intimate or narrative feel.

While still elaborate, the focus shifted slightly from the pure spectacle of a Lagerfeld show to creating an immersive story around the collection.

66

As soon as I receive his sketches, the process begins. I try to please him, but I like to surprise him too.

99

Virginie Viard

Describing her and Lagerfeld's collaborative process, telegraph.co.uk, 20 February 2019

"

She's action versus talk, [Viard] embraces otherness – she herself is quite strange in a beautiful way.

"

Kristen Stewart,

Chanel brand ambassador and actor, on Viard, vogue.co.uk, 6 June 2024

Karl Lagerfeld initiated the first Chanel Métiers d'Art collection in 2001. The annual collection and show celebrate the artisans who contribute to the fashion house.

Chanel started acquiring small ateliers in the 1980s, and the Métiers d'Art collection pays homage to the tradition and innovation embodied by these smaller brands.

66

Because I like everything to be mixed up, all the different eras, between the renaissance and romanticism, between rock and something very girly – it is all very Chanel.

99

Virginie Viard

On the significance of the Métiers d'Art shows, anothermag.com, 4 December 2020

"

Chanel's commitment to its Métiers d'Art is crucial. It's a statement about preserving heritage and the invaluable human skill that underpins true luxury.

"

Imran Amed

Fashion industry expert, on the importance of artisanal crafts, businessoffashion.com, 7 December 2021

Under Viard, the brand of Chanel also adapted to the digital age, embracing online presentations during global events and utilizing social media to connect with a younger, global audience.

The accessories and cosmetic lines continued to thrive.

66

It was Karl's and Gabrielle Chanel's studio – to me it has never been an ordinary workplace.

99

Virginie Viard

On working in the Chanel studio, vogue.com, 27 April 2020

"

Virginie loves luxury in clothing – the craftsmanship, the beauty. But she's always been incredibly practical.

"

Eric Wright

Chanel ambassador and rapper, on Viard, vogue.com, 24 November 2020

Under Viard's direction, the House of Chanel continued its expansion, opening new boutiques and strengthening its global presence.

The brand's focus remained on high-end luxury goods, from ready-to-wear and haute couture to fragrances, beauty, watches and fine jewellery, upholding its position at the pinnacle of the luxury market.

"

Truthfulness and realness will be leading me going forward.

"

Virginie Viard

On her design ethos, vogue.com, 27 April 2020

"

Chanel under Viard is proving that quiet luxury can be just as powerful as grand spectacle. It's a more subtle, yet equally compelling, narrative.

"

Alexander Fury

Fashion critic, on Viard's approach to luxury, theguardian.com, 3 March 2020

The iconic elements of Chanel – the tweed, the camellia, the chain bags, the two-tone shoes and the pearls – remained central to Viard's vision.

Consistently reinterpreting these codes, Viard ensured that they felt fresh for contemporary women while preserving their timeless appeal.

"

Viard's genius lies in her ability to make the iconic feel new again without resorting to overt reinvention. It's a respectful evolution.

"

Dana Thomas

Fashion journalist, on Viard's treatment of Chanel codes, newyorker.com, 27 May 2020

"

It's a dialogue between Coco, Karl and me. I always try to think, 'What would she do now?' or 'What would he want to do now?'

"

Virginie Viard

On her ongoing conversation with her Chanel predecessors, wwd.com, 26 January 2021

"

The challenge for Chanel, and all luxury brands, is to remain aspirational while becoming more accountable. Viard's subtle approach may be key to this balance.

"

Achim Berg

Fashion industry analyst, on Chanel's future challenges, mckinsey.com, 2 March 2021

❝

I feel good when I'm working.
That's my life, that's what I love.

❞

Virginie Viard

On her dedication to her role at Chanel, interviewmagazine.com,
27 May 2020

"

The future of Chanel is in good hands. Viard understands the essence of the brand, and she's bringing a quiet strength that resonates with how women want to dress now.

"

Nicole Phelps

Fashion critic, on the outlook for Chanel under Viard, vogue.com, 27 May 2020

> "
>
> Virginie's vision is so much more about a life and what you wear in it, rather than trying to make statements about fashion or change. They're not concerned in this company with, 'Are we relevant?' They're not torturing themselves. It's much more about supporting the life of the woman who buys her clothes. It's a very feminine approach.
>
> "

Inez van Lamsweerd

Visual artist, on the brand's focus, vogue.com, 24 November 2020

"

It's not just about clothes. It's about a lifestyle, an attitude.

"

Virginie Viard

On the broader impact of the Chanel brand, harpersbazaar.com, 30 September 2021

Viard shocked the fashion world by stepping down as creative director of Chanel in the summer of 2024.

By December, the brand had announced her replacement – French-Belgian designer Matthieu Blazy, who had been creative director at Bottega Veneta since 2021. His debut runway show for Chanel in late 2025 was regarded as a huge success as the industry eagerly embraced this bold new chapter in House of Chanel history.

"

Clutch your pearls. Cover your ears. Talk about a big bang: under a galactic stage set, the designer Matthieu Blazy just blasted the world's most famous fashion brand through the sound barrier and into the 21st century...

"

Jess Cartner-Morley

Fashion journalist, on Blazy's debut runway show at the spring/summer 2026 Paris Fashion Week, theguardian.com, 7 October 2025

"

The myth of Chanel makes her a very serious woman. [But] I found a picture of her with a flamenco dress, having fun. She decided for herself what she could be. The good thing with the codes of Chanel is that you can also reduce them; they still look like Chanel.

"

Matthieu Blazy

On the legacy of Coco Chanel and his reinvention of the brand's classic codes, theindustry.fashion, 7 October 2025

> "
> The creative process begun by Gabrielle Chanel, now eager for redemption and willing to find the future in the foundations of the past, through the hands of Matthieu Blazy.
> "

Alice Abbiadati

Fashion journalist, on Blazy's reinvention of Chanel, voguearabia.com, 7 October 2025

CHAPTER
FIVE

KEY DESIGNS

THE HOUSE OF CHANEL IS
RESPONSIBLE FOR SOME OF THE
MOST-WORN DESIGNS OF THE
TWENTIETH AND TWENTY-FIRST
CENTURIES.

HERE WE BREAK DOWN THE
MOST IMPORTANT DESIGNS
OF THE FASHION HOUSE, FROM
THEIR CREATION TO THEIR
MODERN-DAY EVOLUTION.

The **Little Black Dress** (LBD), often attributed to Coco Chanel, became a symbol of democratic elegance.

First popularized by Chanel in the 1920s, it offered a versatile, sophisticated and accessible dress option for women of all walks of life.

While the LBD has been copied and re-imagined by many designers over the years, they all have Coco to thank.

"

Black, like white, is the best colour.
They both look great with added
colour touches like red.

"

Karl Lagerfeld

On the LBD's signature colour, elle.com, 19 February 2019

"

I imposed black; it's still going strong today, for black wipes out everything else around.

"

Coco Chanel

On the dominance of the colour black, wwd.com,
27 August 2024

"

Chanel was, as we know, a problematic character, but her gift for self-promotion, and her nous for assessing the precise tipping point for a style, allowed her to position herself as the visionary behind the LBD.

"

Lauren Cochrane

Fashion writer, on Coco Chanel's LBD revolution,
The Ten: The Stories Behind the Fashion Classics, 2021

"

Luxury is to spend a lot on what you really don't need. But it's an industry and there's nothing bad about that. I prefer to make clothes [rather] than arms. Maybe you can be dressed to kill... but dresses, they don't kill anybody.

"

Karl Lagerfeld

On the meaning of luxury and the LBD, vogue.co.uk, 4 November 2015

Now a chic addition to any wardrobe, when Chanel was designing the LBD, black was reserved for those in mourning, as well as the lower classes, servants and shop girls.

The creation of the LBD came after the end of World War I, and Chanel supposedly drew inspiration from her own personal loss – the tragic passing of her lover and business partner Arthur "Boy" Capel in 1919.

"

One is never over-dressed
or underdressed with a Little
Black Dress.

"

Karl Lagerfeld

On the LBD, ca.style.yahoo.com, 11 March 2023

"

The best colour in the whole world
is the one that looks good on you.

"

Coco Chanel

On choosing your colours, instyle.com, 11 January 2024

The **Chanel suit**, with its signature tweed fabric, braid trim and collarless jacket, was reinvented in 1945 as part of Coco Chanel's comeback collection.

Designed for movement and comfort, it offered a chic and practical alternative to the restrictive fashions of the mid-twentieth century. Lagerfeld later reimagined the jacket once again for a contemporary audience, firmly mainting the Chanel suit's timeless legacy.

"

The suit is the answer to the modern woman's need to be chic and move freely.

"

Coco Chanel

On the practicality and elegance of her suit design, chanel.com, 7 July 2025

"

The idea is to take the most iconic jacket of the twentieth century and make it in a way that couldn't have been made until the twenty-first.

"

Karl Lagerfeld

On his modernization of the classic Chanel jacket, using the original as a moodboard, vogue.co.uk, 4 November 2015

> **"**
>
> Put on an original Chanel jacket and you feel like you've stepped into a silken hug… It feels like love. Put on a Lagerfeld jacket and note the difference. In the mirror you might look better: figure more defined, vibe more modern.
>
> **"**

Rhonda Garelick

Fashion writer, on the two jacket styles, thecut.com, 19 February 2019

"

If I ruled the world, every woman would have a Chanel suit in her wardrobe.

"

Bill Nighy

Actor, on the classic Chanel suit, theguardian.com, 4 July 2010

From the Chanel suit came the **Chanel jacket**.

Once part of the two-piece set, Lagerfeld dramatically reinterpreted the Chanel jacket, adding modern elements, distressed finishes and unexpected materials, while Virginie Viard brought a lighter, more relaxed sensibility to its silhouette, making it versatile for contemporary wear.

The original Chanel jacket included a small chain sewn into the hem to ensure it hung perfectly and maintained its shape, a subtle but ingenious detail for impeccable drape.

The **2.55 handbag**, named for its creation date, February 1955, revolutionized women's accessories.

Coco Chanel, tired of carrying her bag in her hands, designed a quilted leather bag with a long chain strap, allowing it to be carried on the shoulder, thus freeing the hands.

Reimagined by Lagerfeld, Viard and Blazy, the 2.55 remains one of the most recognisable bags to this day.

"

Luxury is something very few people have… And to buy a handbag is to have a dream of getting nearer. That's our culture and tons of people – me included – make a lot of money from it.

"

Karl Lagerfeld

Discussing the appeal of the luxury brand, as manifested in the handbag, nytimes.com, 12 October 2015

The burgundy leather lining of the original 2.55 bag was reportedly inspired by the colour of the uniforms worn by the nuns at the orphanage where Coco Chanel lived from age 11.

In each 2.55 bag there is also a secret pocket inside the front flap – allegedly first designed for Coco to hide her love letters!

The **two-tone shoe**, another feature of Chanel's post-war oeuvre, was first introduced in 1957.

Featuring a beige body with a black toe cap, Chanel is said to have designed the shoe to create the illusion of a lengthened leg and shortened foot, with the black toe protecting against scuffs.

Blazy softened the two-tone shoe for his debut show, moulding the leather around the foot to add a new layer of comfort to Chanel.

"

A woman with good shoes
is never ugly.

"

Coco Chanel

On the importance of footwear, wwd.com, 27 August 2024

The **camellia** is Chanel's emblematic flower, derived from Coco Chanel's personal fascination with its geometric perfection and lack of scent, making it an ideal, discreet accessory.

Lagerfeld continued with the motif of the camellia flower in many of his collections, most notably his Chanel couture debut in 1984 where they appeared on hats and headpieces.

Blazy also included camellia buttons and embroidery in his debut show.

> So synonymous with the house is the camellia, it's essentially interchangeable with the interlocking 'CC' logo stamp. With its plump, rounded head of perfectly symmetrical petals and its dark, glossy leaves, the botanical Chanel icon is a beguiling one.

Clare McInerney

Fashion writer, on Chanel's use of the camellia, voguescandinavia.com, 15 April 2024

The **pearl necklace**, particularly the long, layered strands favoured by Coco Chanel, became a signature accessory, often paired with her simple jersey dresses in the1920s or tweed suits from the 1950s.

Her innovative approach made costume jewellery fashionable, blurring the lines between real and imitation and emphasizing style over preciousness.

"

Adornment, what a science!
Beauty, what a weapon! Modesty,
what elegance!

"

Coco Chanel

On the powers of appearance, townandcountrymag.com,
16 August 2017

Coco Chanel famously mixed real pearls among fake ones, a radical idea for her time.

She believed that the style and how you wore the jewellery mattered more than its inherent value.

This mixture of high and low accessories can also be seen in Lagerfeld's work.

The annual Chanel Métiers d'Art show, formalized by Karl Lagerfeld, celebrates the unparalleled craftsmanship of the specialized ateliers Chanel has acquired (like Lesage for embroidery, Massaro for shoes).

These collections showcase the extraordinary artisanal skills that bring Chanel's designs to life, ensuring the preservation of rare crafts such as high-end accessory and shoemaking.

> "
> Collections are all very well, but I need to be moved. It has to be alive, it has to connect to other disciplines.
> "

Virginie Viard

On the importance of supporting Chanel's Métiers d'Art, wwd. com, 8 December 2022

Each Métiers d'Art collection is dedicated to a specific city that inspired Coco Chanel or Karl Lagerfeld, from New York and Rome to Hamburg and Dakar, blending the historical with artisanal excellence, as well as trasnporting fashion beyond its typical epicentres of Paris and London.

66

I don't understand how a woman can leave the house without fixing herself up a little – if only out of politeness. And then, you never know, maybe that's the day she has a date with destiny. And it's best to be as pretty as possible for destiny.

99

Coco Chanel

On the importance of appearance, instyle.com,
11 January 2024

Introduced by Karl Lagerfeld in 2011, the **Boy Chanel bag** pays homage to Coco Chanel's first great love, Arthur "Boy" Capel, as well as her tomboyish spirit.

It represents a more edgy, structured and overtly masculine-inspired aesthetic compared to the classic 2.55, and appeals to a younger, more fashion-forward clientele.

"

Chanel used men's underwear to make dresses; she had this boyish attitude, in fact, it is the very spirit of Chanel. She got it from Boy Capel.

"

Karl Lagerfeld

On the inspiration behind the Boy Chanel bag, rebag.com, 29 July 2020

Chanel's **double "C" logo** has never been changed.

Created in 1925 by Coco herself, the globally recognizable design is one of only a handful of logos to have never been updated – such is its distinctiveness.

CHAPTER
SIX

ICONIC CHANEL MOMENTS

SINCE ITS INCEPTION, THE HOUSE OF CHANEL HAS BEEN INFUSED WITH THE GLITZ AND GLAMOUR OF THE STARS OF THE LAST CENTURY. FROM FIRST LADIES TO RAPPERS, ARISTOCRATS TO ACTORS, CHANEL HAS PERMEATED EVERY CORNER OF POPULAR CULTURE FOR OVER ONE HUNDRED YEARS.

In 1931, Hollywood came knocking on Coco Chanel's door. With movie attendance down as a result of the Great Depression, Samuel Goldwyn of MGM Studios turned to Chanel to create striking costumes and red-carpet looks for the studio's stars.

However, Chanel's minimalist aesthetic clashed with what the audiences were expecting.

66

A woman can be overdressed but never over elegant.

99

Coco Chanel

On the importance of appearance, townandcountrymag,com, 16 August 2017

66

[Hollywood] was like an evening at the Folies Bergère*. Once it is agreed that the girls were beautiful in their feathers there is not much to add.

99

Coco Chanel

On being unimpressed by Hollywood, vanityfair.com, 8 February 2017

* A Parisien music hall

The influence of Chanel was felt on and off-screen. Actresses such as Greta Garbo and Gloria Swanson wore Chanel on the red carpet.

The New York department of Chanel was incredibly profitable in the 1930s – illustrating the brand's popularity with wealthy Manhattanites.

"

Real chic means being well-dressed,
but not conspicuously dressed.
I abhor eccentricity.

"

Coco Chanel

Explaining why she didn't feel that Hollywood was a good fit for
her design sensibilities, interview with *The New York Times*, 1931,
vanityfair.com, 8 February 2017

Future Hollywood designers would pay homage to Chanel – the most notable of which was fellow French designer Hubert de Givenchy.

Drawing on the classic elegance of the Chanel Little Black Dress, Givenchy created one of cinema's most recognizable looks: the black *Breakfast at Tiffany's* dress.

"

The little black dress is the hardest thing to realise, because you must keep it simple.

"

Hubert de Givenchy

On the complex refinement of a LBD, created by Chanel, nytimes.com, 12 March 2018

It could be said that one of Coco Chanel's most timeless contributions to popular culture is not her designs at all – but Chanel No. 5.

The perfume transcended its status as a mere fragrance to become a cultural touchstone. Its presence in literature, film and art cemented its mystique and positioned it as a symbol of luxury and feminine allure.

66

I only wear Chanel No. 5.

99

Marilyn Monroe

When asked what she wore to bed – an iconic endorsement,
Life Magazine, 7 April 1952

Marilyn Monroe became an overnight ambassador for Chanel No. 5 after a quip to a cheeky journalist who enquired about her sleeping arrangements.

In 2012, archival footage of Monroe speaking about Chanel No. 5 was used for an advertisement for the perfume, illustrating its timeless appeal.

"

A woman who doesn't wear perfume has no future.

Coco Chanel

On the importance of scent, wwd.com, 27 August 2024

Andy Warhol famously created a series of silkscreen pop art prints featuring the Chanel No. 5 bottle in the 1980s, further immortalizing the perfume and its iconic status.

The Chanel suit became a powerful symbol of sophisticated femininity and career women in the mid-twentieth century.

Former first lady Jacqueline Kennedy famously wore a pink Chanel suit on the day of John F. Kennedy's assassination, forever imbuing the garment with historical significance and a poignant place in American popular culture.

"

Oh, no… I want them to see what they have done to Jack.

"

Jacqueline Kennedy Onassis

When asked if she wanted to remove her blood-stained Chanel suit after the assassination of John F. Kennedy, *Coco Chanel: The Legend and the Life*, Justine Picardie, 2010

"

My suits are made for the woman who lives, who travels, who works.

"

Coco Chanel

On the active lifestyle her suits were designed for, chanel.com, 7 July 2025

While Coco birthed the brand, it was Karl Lagerfeld who truly turned Chanel into an unrivalled cultural force.

Lagerfeld's ability to infuse pop culture references and celebrity power into Chanel's DNA was unparalleled. He brought music legends, Hollywood stars and fashion's new guard into his campaigns and onto his runways, making Chanel *the* designer for the contemporary celebrity era.

"

So to survive you have to cut the roots to make new roots. Because fashion is about today. You can take an idea from the past, but, if you do it the way it was, no one wants it.

"

Karl Lagerfeld

Defending his decisions when faced with criticism of how he modernized the brand, newyorker.com, 12 March 2007

Karl Lagerfeld cultivated close relationships with numerous celebrities, including Kristen Stewart, Pharrell Williams and Cara Delevingne, who became modern-day muses and ambassadors for the brand, bridging the gap between high fashion and mainstream appeal.

"

When Kendall [Jenner] was walking in his [Lagerfeld's] shows all the time, he would say to her, 'Please give this to your mother', and send me gifts. He was always so supportive of her, and he always remembered me. He was the kindest and most generous man.

"

Kris Jenner

On her family's connection to Chanel and Karl, vogue.co.uk, 23 February 2019

66

I like to give people something
to talk about. A show should be
a moment, an event.

99

Karl Lagerfeld

On the theatricality of his star-studded Chanel presentations,
interviewmagazine.com, 1 October 2010

The Chanel supermarket set for the Autumn/Winter 2014 show featured 500,000 custom-made Chanel-branded products, from milk cartons to doormats, all created specifically for the show.

The show closed with Lagerfeld walking arm in arm with supermodel of the moment, Cara Delevingne.

"

The only thing more inspiring than Karl's vision, talent and creativity was his heart. He was one of the first designers I worked with in Paris, and that initial collaboration – and every time we worked together since – shaped my perspective of the fashion industry.

"

Karlie Kloss

Chanel model and favourite of Lagerfeld, vogue.co.uk, 23 February 2019

"

It's an opportunity for Chanel
to continue to lead for the next
20 years.

"

Bruno Pavlovsky

Chanel's president of fashion, on the change of guard after
Viard's exit, voguebusiness.com, 12 December 2024

Chanel remains constantly namechecked in music across genres and generations with a recent example being Bad Bunny's collaboration with Eladio Carrión, entitled "Coco Chanel", whose lyrics pay tribute to the brand's founder.

Today, Chanel continues to blend with popular culture through its celebrity ambassadors, digital content and collaborations, albeit with a more understated approach than in the Lagerfeld era.

The brand remains a fixture on red carpets and at high-profile events, maintaining its desirability among the world's most influential figures. With Blazy at the helm, one can only guess at what the next evolution of Chanel will be.

> **"** His vision and talent will reinforce the energy of the brand and our position as a leader in luxury. **"**

Leena Nair

Global CEO of Chanel, on Matthieu Blazy's appointment, voguebusiness.com, 12 December 2024

66

Improvise. Become more creative. Not because you have to, but because you want to. Evolution is the secret for the next step.

99

Karl Lagerfeld

Words of wisdom that Coco Chanel would surely approve of, harpersbazaar.com, 19 February 2020